AN ARCHITECT IN ITALY

An Architect in Italy

Caroline Mauduit

with a Foreword by
Sir Hugh Casson

Clarkson N. Potter, Inc./Publishers
Distributed by Crown Publishers, Inc., New York

To P.A.

Foreword

THIS is a lovely book, observant, informative, elegant, true. True because the author-artist Caroline Mauduit is an architect, treating buildings with knowledge and respect, knowing how they are put together, how and where weight is transferred, how tensions are expressed, how ornament is used to punctuate and enrich. This gives all her drawings authority as well as information. She has discovered too that there is no better way of understanding, enjoying and remembering a building than to draw—ever at pains to measure it. (Her sketching equipment, she tells us, always includes a measuring tape.)

Thus what captivates the reader's attention is not just the sharpness of her observation and the elegance of her drawing but her power to think in section and in plan as she reads what she sees. Modestly she calls this book 'a working record' of her time in Rome. Engagingly she confesses that gradually the wish to compose each page grew stronger as she worked . . . and quite right too as the results so clearly show. She writes as she draws, simply and directly, with true love for her subjects.

She obviously enjoyed every minute of her voyage of discovery and so do we.

Hugh Casson

Author's Acknowledgements

I would like to thank everyone at the British School in Rome, especially the Director, Professor Donald Bullough, the Assistant Director, Amanda Claridge, and the Secretary, Maria Pia Malvezzi; the many friends I made in Rome, both English and Italian; the Bartlett School of Architecture, University College, London, where I was able to acquire the habit of visiting foreign parts through the generosity of their travelling scholarships; Sir Hugh Casson and my fellow architects and friends at Ramsay Tugwell Associates; Adam Nicolson, for his help and enthusiasm; all at 15 Savile Row; my husband, Brian, for everything; and lastly my father, who shared his love of architecture with me and nurtured it from an early age.

Endpapers: From Giambattista Nolli's Nuova pianta di Roma, *1748, by permission of the Syndics of Cambridge University Library.*

Published in the United States by Clarkson N. Potter, Inc., 225 Park Avenue South, New York, New York 10003, and represented in Canada by the Canadian MANDA Group.

Published in Great Britain by Bloomsbury Publishing Limited.

CLARKSON N. POTTER, POTTER, and colophon are trademarks of Clarkson N. Potter, Inc.

Printed in Spain by Cayfosa, Barcelona

Library of Congress Cataloging-in-Publication Data
Mauduit, Caroline.
An Architect in Italy.
1. Architecture, Renaissance – Italy – Rome. 2. Architecture – Italy – Rome. 3. Rome (Italy) – Buildings, structures, etc. 4. Architecture, Renaissance – Italy. 5. Architecture – Italy. 6. Classicism in architecture – Italy. I. Title.
NA1120.M38   1988   720'.945   88-4080
ISBN 0-517-56980-9

10 9 8 7 6 5 4 3 2

Contents

Introduction

This book began on a cold February morning in London. I was in my final diploma year at the Bartlett School of Architecture —it was 1983—when I saw, pinned up on the main noticeboard, a piece of paper headed 'The Rome Scholarship in Architecture'. Every year, it said, the British School in Rome awards the scholarship to an architectural student who wants to spend the following year in Italy. It was exactly what I wanted to do. I have always been interested in the relationship of architecture to landscape and I decided to apply to the board to study those Italian villas and gardens which had intrigued Napoleon's architects, Percier and Fontaine. Armed with my portfolio, a sketchbook with which I had travelled the previous summer in eastern Europe, and a very old Baedeker, I went— rather apprehensively—to the selection interview. Fifteen grand old men of architecture interviewed me and, to my amazement and delight, decided in the end to offer me the scholarship.

I drove out to Italy in October 1983. The imposing white façade of the British School in Rome (by Lutyens, using elements from the west front of St Paul's) overlooks the Borghese Gardens. The school was set up at the turn of the century for archaeologists but in 1911 it was expanded to give students of architecture, sculpture and painting facilities to match the French and American academies in Rome.

It is a wonderful institution, full of oddities and eccentrics —classical and medieval scholars, archaeologists, artists, art historians, sculptors, painters—a rich mixture of personalities all managing somehow to live under one roof. Everyone does what they want to do during the day—working in the library or in one of the studios at the back, or going to look at something in the middle of Rome—and then in the evening they all meet up for supper in hall, with a blazing fire at one end and Reno serving pasta on a silver tray. It was then that the British School would come into its own. At supper I would always learn something new or extraordinary—that the Romans used to preserve the stone of their statues with sour milk; that the Arch of Septimius Severus had been intact until this century when the exhaust smoke from the bus park next door virtually destroyed it; that archaeologists—in private—are still completely uncertain about the actual history of the Roman Forum. For all of that, more than anything else, I will be eternally grateful to the British School, especially to Donald Bullough, who was Director when I was there; Amanda Claridge, the Assistant Director, whose knowledge is inexhaustible and generous; and Maria Pia Malvezzi, the secretary and arranger extraordinaire, who knows all the conceivable ins and outs of Italian bureaucracy and who managed to get me into all sorts of places which would otherwise have been impossible.

So here I was, as perfectly set up as anyone could hope for. I had a large room on the first floor above the painters' studios at the back of the School, looking out over a mimosa tree. I was fed every night. I was free for a year. I had a car and could travel the length and breadth of Italy. And of course, best of all, at my very doorstep, a short walk across the Borghese Gardens, there was Rome itself. I had been there before but it had never been a great success. My parents had dragged me round Italy when I was ten. The endless cathedrals, galleries and villas had not gone down well and I spent the entire holiday complaining about the plumbing and the filth. This time it was different. Like everyone else, I suppose, I fell in love with Rome. An opera singer gave me a pale pink bicycle, with a pink basket to match, and on this I made my way around, gradually sorting out the layers of this extraordinary *millefeuilles* of a city. My sketchbook went with me everywhere, along with a watercolour box, a bottle of water and a measuring tape. Often I wandered at will, following my nose, and was rewarded by a glimpse here and there of a hidden cloister, a beautiful garden or a strange fountain. Whenever I saw something that interested me, it was committed to a page of the sketchbook.

Drawing a building is a way of remembering it properly. To draw you have to look very hard and I think it is in the looking itself that the building is impressed on the mind. Often I measured it and made a plan, putting the dimensions on the drawing, because I know from experience that only by doing that can I understand what I am looking at. In this way, I didn't set out to make the sketchbook anything more than a working record, but gradually the decorative urge to fill every available space and the need to compose the page took over. The pattern on each of the pages slowly became an end in itself.

So that is the genesis of the book: at first incidental and casual, gradually more deliberate and arranged. It is, in a way, a visual diary, as spontaneous and haphazard as that, but governed all the time by one overriding aim: to try and understand the architecture of Renaissance Italy. It is extraordinarily

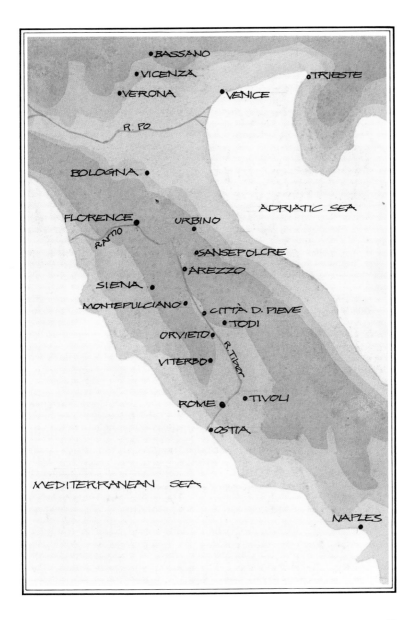

difficult to put an understanding of buildings into words. Like music, architecture is an art which in some ways bypasses words. All façades tell a story (a story which can only be about themselves) and it is the meaning of those stories which this sketchbook tries to approach. It is the great miracle of the classical language of architecture developed in Renaissance Italy that the arrangement of brick and stone and stucco can convey as many meanings as music or poetry. Too much of the classical revival now underway has forgotten this. It is formalist and polite in tone, as though the classical language were a building's equivalent of the tail coat and top hat. You only have to *look* at the buildings of Renaissance Italy to see that to reduce it to that is to make a boring travesty out of one of the greatest means of expression ever developed.

In all my exploring I was helped immeasurably by the crowd of enthusiasts at the School. It would not have been the same without them. The only drawback was that I found myself cocooned in a little English society of its own. This made it rather difficult to meet Italians and I decided after nine months to leave the School and share the flat of a friend of mine, Jane Boreham. It was small but beautiful, right in the middle, deeply embedded in the medieval part of Rome near the Campo dei Fiori, with log beams and clay tiles on the roof, like a Tuscan cottage perched on the rooftops. There were probably a million others like ours which had glorious views over the roofs, terraces and domes to the Alban Hills beyond the city, but of course it always felt as if you were alone. The bells of the church next door seemed to peal constantly. Every morning they woke us up and every evening they rang for the angelus, that great moment in the day when all the bells of Rome are rung, calling people to evening prayers. High up on our secret terrace we would look down on the hubbub of the Italian world, with its noisy scooters, gesticulating inhabitants, children going to school and slow-moving women setting off to buy vegetables.

The day began with breakfast in the local café—a cappuccino and cornetto. The morning was usually spent sketching—this is what I wanted to do more than anything else and it was reassuring to know that I could just about keep myself by selling a watercolour here and there. After an exhausting morning with pen and brush—people will *never* understand that it is actually hard work looking and drawing—I might meet a few friends in a café for lunch. Then I could go home to the flat for the siesta and continue with drawing in the cooler part of the evening. After supper I sometimes used to meet some Italian friends for a *dopocena*, a party late at night which more often than not would be outside, eating ice-cream and talking under the stars until the small hours of the next day. It was a perfect, indulgent, civilized way of life which after three more months I felt I had to bring to an end to face the reality of finding a job in an architect's practice in London.

CAROLINE MAUDUIT

1988

Easter Sunday.

Ancient Rome

S. Peters for Bernini's balcony.

14 Arbour in Forum

The Forum

15

I still rather wish there were cows and sheep grazing in the Forum. Archaeology tends to strip away the romance of a place. All the same, it is quite easy in Rome to find some ruins which have that 18th-century dilettante air about them. You will hardly find it in the Forum, where the archaeologists have dug and redug, but you will only a few yards away on the edge of the Palatine. I often came to wander here with one or two friends under the olives and umbrella pines. Everywhere you look the ruined blocks emerge casually from the grass. Wild fennel and acanthus leaves brush against the fragments of a giant architrave, where the egg and dart moulding is cut six inches into the marble—more precisely and richly done than anything from the fifth century to the fifteenth.

Suddenly, in that one detail, you get an idea of the vast scale of Imperial Rome and exactly how ostentatious it must have been. And then, again, on top of that, another layer: the real excitement of someone like Alberti or Brunelleschi poking around among the ruins, finding these Roman details for the first time.

Egg and dart moulding.

Down in the Forum itself, draped in the wistaria of Easter Sunday and only a yard or two from where Cicero and Crassus both had their houses, I painted the Sacred Way (p. 15) sitting on a shady bench in an arbour and listening to the bronze Roman doors of the Temple of Romulus creaking on their hinges.

All this is very different from the dark remains of Nero's Golden House (p. 19). This huge palace was buried by Trajan, Nero's successor as Emperor, who loathed extravagance and selfishness. (The portrait bust of Nero in the Capitoline, with his disgusting elongated sideboards, is all you ever need to see to know the character of the man.) The Golden House, in the familiar Italian way, has been closed for restorations for decades, but with special permission I managed to get in. You have to take a torch and you can't see anything around you except when its light glimpses some delicate Roman painting in Pompeian style, exactly as Raphael would have seen it when he was lowered down here on a rope to inspect the miraculously preserved frescoes. The great central dining room even in its present dank and mossy state is able to impress with its style and sophistication, a niche on every facet, perspectives disappearing down the corridors.

Of course, the Golden House is rather an exception. Most of the ancient remains in Rome are much more casually to hand. That is one part of the theatricality of the city—the way in which the massive and enormously old is so coolly announced. We have dinner on the pavement opposite the Pantheon (pp. 26–7), nearly indifferent to its vast granite portico, each column of which—eighteen of them—was transported on a separate ship from Egypt at the beginning of the second century. Or, near the heavy, crusted stonework of the Theatre of Marcellus (medieval flats squeezed into a Roman theatre) washing is draped like bunting in front of a Roman gate, the Portico d'Ottavia (pp. 20–21), built by Augustus in 23 BC for his sister. Here more than anywhere else you get the feeling of the ancient classical remains used as a shell for medieval dwellings. This is the real texture of Rome. Thank goodness—for once—the Portico has not been stripped clean and restored.

One develops an eye for imaginative reconstructions of the ruins. I became fascinated by the Markets of Trajan (pp. 22–23). They are not only a classic piece of town planning, but precise and subtle in the way that a very large building of many small parts can be made to work. This enormous 2nd-century development of 150 new shops and offices was connected to libraries, a basilica and Trajan's column itself. On the first-floor entablature which runs the length of the wide semicircle of shops, Trajan's architect Apollodorus has played a subtle and almost mannerist fugue on the three varieties of pediment— broken, triangular and segmental—all of them in hand-carved brick which was rubbed into shape. Each shop window has been given an identity but each is visibly part of a larger scheme.

Below Orti Farnesiana, overlooking the Forum

Pantheon.

A

B

C

A B

C

18

Pantheon

Nero's Golden House

roman concrete

Octagonal room.
? Triclinium

Filippino Lippi 1457–1504
Ritratto de Vecchio

Giovanni Bellini
1430 · 1516
Ritratto di Gentiluomo

Lorenzo di Credi
1459–1537 Venere.

21

ehind Portico d' Ottavia.

20

Portico d'Ottavia.

21

Trajans market

2

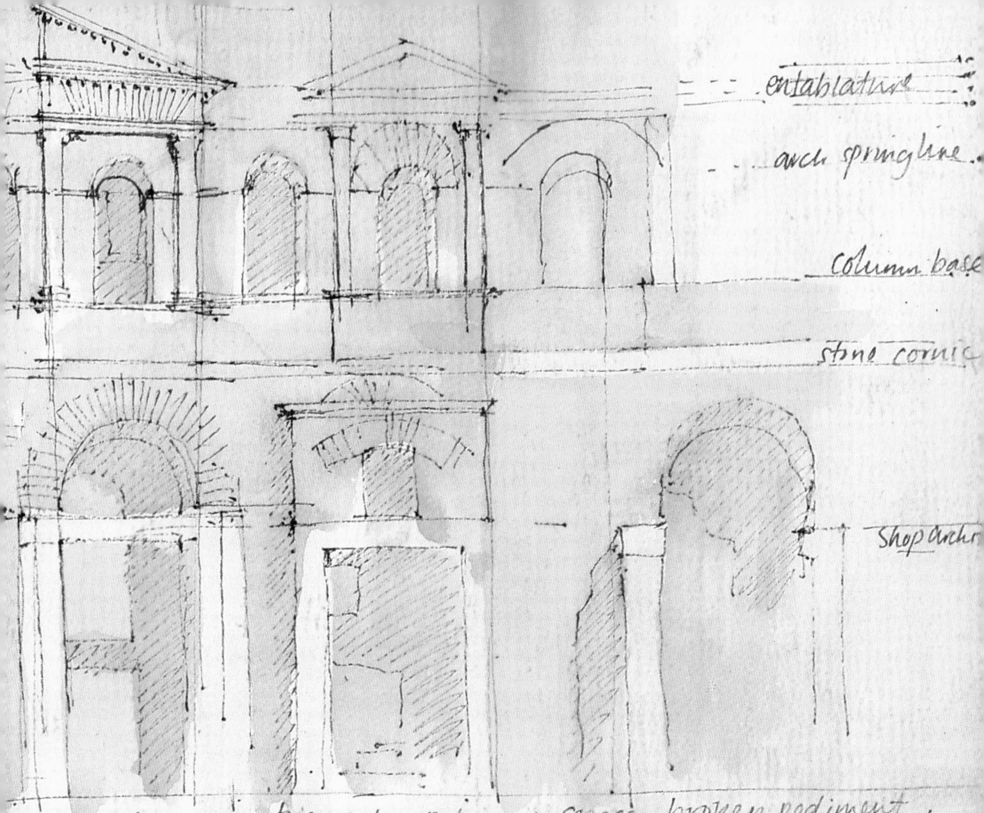

entablature

arch springline

column base

stone cornice

Shop arch

hen pediment, space, triangular pediment, space, broken pediment,
ace, segmental pediment, space, broken pediment

23

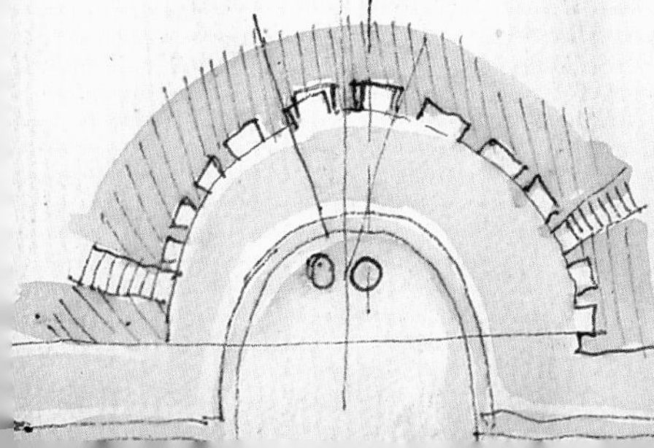

Sperlonga   Tiberius's villa. CIBC — extended by Augustu
sculpture   Grotto.   Sylla = Polyphemus. — Same author as
museum.   appropriateness to Grotto.   Rhodian Sc

sailor ——▽
grabbing onto
ships
mast

1 of 6 of Syllas dog heads
eating a sailor.

Roman →
er dovecotes
den Whitehouse.
logical Review.

Terrachina

OSTIA

mithras slaying bull Ostia

25

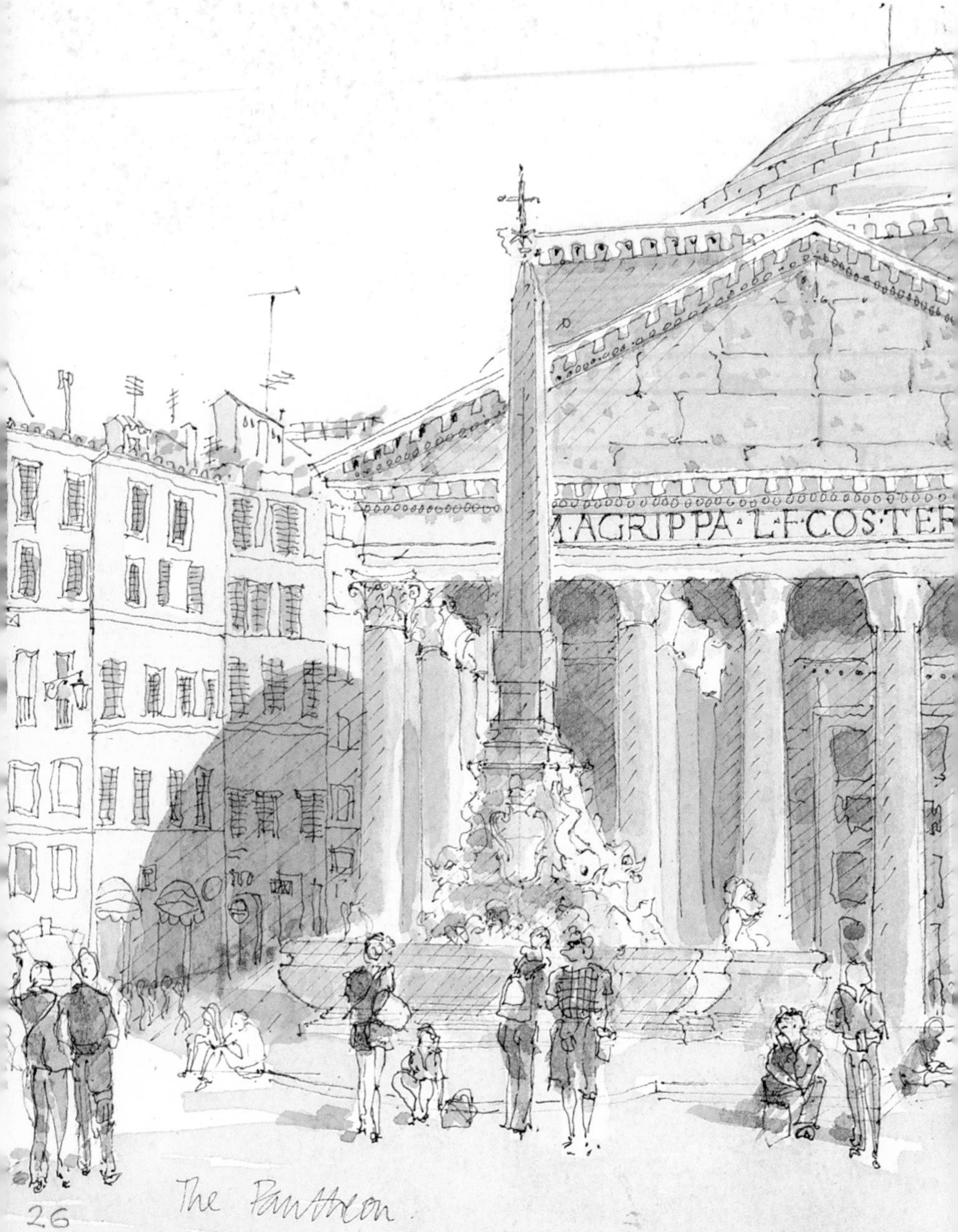
M AGRIPPA L F COS TER

The Pantheon.

Renaissance Rome

IF you arrive in Rome at night, you should take a taxi to the Piazza del Popolo (pp. 28–29). It is the best place to begin; it was where I always got off the bus from the British School. The piazza is a set, a stage entrance. The great oval expanse was laid out with neoclassical precision by Giuseppe Valadier in 1823. In the centre is an ancient Egyptian obelisk and the rather wimpish, camel-like lions of Valadier's fountains.

At the far end, on either side of the entrance to the Corso, is a pair of baroque churches, commissioned by Pope Alexander in 1660 from Carlo Rainaldi. Even though the sites are of different widths, Rainaldi has ingeniously made them appear symmetrical by giving S. Maria di Monte Santo (on the left) an oval dome, and S. Maria de' Miracoli a round one. But more than this, it's the idea of *twin* churches that is so original. The mere fact of doubling a church is lavish and extravagant. As a solution for the monumental entrance to a city it is unequalled. It integrates, in Rome of all places, the idea of the church and the city. It makes the church the key to the city. But unlike a single grand temple in such a place, there is nothing in this piece of theatrical town-planning which stops you, which tells you that you have arrived. On the contrary, there is movement and drama in the whole arrangement and, like a pair of courtiers bowing to your entrance, the two churches are pulled slightly back and turned inwards, the grandest pair of theatre curtains ever made.

Popolo is the perfect baroque setting. For its rococo equal go straight down the Corso, past the string of palaces and glossy shops, to find the Piazza S. Ignazio (pp. 32–33) just off to the right. Here in 1727 an architect with the wonderfully rococo name of Raguzzini laid out the square. There is none of the grand drama of Popolo here, but many exits and entrances, creating little islands of buildings, each with delicately and discreetly curved surfaces mirroring each other across the narrow streets. It is playful and domestic, but still chic and theatrical, as near as architecture can come to grand furniture, and all—crucially—in the scuffed ochre of the semi-neglected Roman stucco.

I have begun at the wrong end. As great a span of time separates us from Raguzzini as him from Bramante. And it is with Bramante that the Renaissance begins in Rome. There are two places that really count—one a staircase in the Vatican, the other the smallest church in the city.

Bramante built the Tempietto (p. 41) in 1502 on the traditional site of St Peter's martyrdom. It is high on a hill on the west bank of the Tiber in the cloister of S. Pietro in Montorio. A little round Doric temple is squeezed into the cloister. It has the perfection of secrecy, of the hidden thing, of too much in too small a space. But more than that it takes—for the first time in Rome—the classical vocabulary, which it uses precisely, and extends it, making a Christian shrine with the grammar of a pagan temple. There is also something critical about its size. It is a building poised exactly between temple and altar.

Not far away in the Vatican, and you must get a special *permesso* to see this, is Bramante's staircase (p. 37). It was part of a much larger scheme, made in the very first years of the sixteenth century, to link the papal apartments with the Belvedere Villa, but of all Bramante's work here it alone has remained untouched. It is a spiral staircase—or more strictly a ramp—climbing 65 feet in five easy turns. It is open to the air and almost unvisited, a dusty place, without the luxurious marble sheen in which so much of the Vatican is coated. There is a certain rough, hand-made quality about it.

Nevertheless, there is an astonishingly inventive piece of architectural drama here. The spiral is supported by 40 columns. As you climb the ramp, you move through the five orders of architecture— one order per turn of the spiral—from Doric, through Tuscan, Ionic, and Corinthian before arriving at the Composite at the top, an order invented by the Romans and considered by them to be the peak of perfection. The first time I visited this staircase it was a sunny day in December. From the loggia at the top the domes of the churches in the city were the only outlines on the haze and far below me, next to a fountain in the form of a galleon, a gardener was digging the papal onions.

32 S. Ignazio

33

34 Bramante's Nymphaeum Genazzano

35

Casa del Cardinale
Bessarione.

Columbarium - Tom

Window higher.

Palazzo Vidoni

36

1·54·914
·27
104
0·88

284

A

B

1st years of (16)

Bramante Staircas
The Vatican

"A"

10
20

10

B

20

Doric order · Paestum.

37

michaelangelo window

"S. Peters"

Early Christian tombs
Under St. Peters

Tomb Kaitainy

15 Via Rusticucci, Vaticano

Palazzo of Giacomo Brecciano

38   124   248   124   246   124   220   121   234   120   235   090

Peruzzi
Palazzo Massimo

Pantheon

Palazzo Massimo 39

Palazzo Pamphili - Piazza Navona 1650

ALARVM TIK

UMBRA

PIAZZA NAVONA

SUB

S. Agnese

40

Tempietto di Bramante & Pietro in Montorio

Plan

Section

PALACES are packed into Rome. Some streets are made of nothing else. Most of the time one is shut out by their deliberately forbidding facades but there is nothing better on a cold winter day than to spend a morning in the warmth and luxury of one of these palaces. My favourites in Rome are Peruzzi's Palazzo Massimo (p. 39), one of the state rooms exquisitely painted with scenes of the Nile, where the pyramids are set against a deep, starry, indigo sky; and the Palazzo Pamphili (p. 40) in the Piazza Navona. Here the white-coated servants of the Brazilian Embassy, which it now is, lead one through room after room until you finally arrive at Borromini's grand *salone*.

These palaces—in fact every classical urban palace built in the last 400 years, from Leningrad to Buenos Aires—are descendants of a house Bramante built for himself in Rome and which Raphael later occupied. It has long since been demolished but just around the corner from S. Andrea della Valle in the Palazzo Vidoni (p. 36) you can still find a building very close to Bramante's original. Everything about it is designed to compliment the High Renaissance grandee. The system of proportion and the classical orders have been grasped and used in the most precise of ways. The solidity of the rusticated basement makes for a firm foundation. The twinned columns, between the windows, establish a simple rhythm along the face of the building, giving it an air of expansiveness and nobility. Above that, the rooms of various dependants recede in grandeur.

The two poles of Renaissance Rome are palaces and gardens. One is completely urban, the other an escape from the city, one part of the traffic and the *press* of Rome, the other its absence, its almost unvisited quiet. The beauty of the three little oratories next to S. Gregorio Magno (p. 44) is at least as much in their being pushed up out of the way in a quiet little grassy arena as in the ingenuity of their architecture. In the seventeenth century three separate buildings (one of them a 3rd-century house!) were fused together here into a trinity of chapels. It is a lovely place. Gaggles of nuns emerge now and then from the convent next door in their white and blue. There are cypresses and oleanders. And, above all this are the associations with

St Gregory the Great. Here he gave bread to the poor and to the angels. On this site he founded the Benedictines. And from here, as a plaque in the church says, he sent out Augustine to convert the English.

Just across the road from S. Gregorio are the Orti Farnesiana on the Palatine. These pleasure gardens were laid out by Vignola in the 1560s for Cardinal Alessandro Farnese. The site was once the centre of the world, the palaces of the Roman Emperors. The walks and gravel paths conceal ancient rooms from which colonies were acquired, assassinations ordered and client kings casually betrayed.

At the northern end of the garden, where you can look out over the Forum to the vaults of the Basilica of Maxentius (known affectionately in the British School as the Bas. Max.), you will find, rather neglected and in a half-ruinous state, parts of Vignola's scheme. The lower half of the terraced garden, with its grand ramp and nymphaeum, has been—quite iniquitously—dug away by the excavators in the Forum. All that has been salvaged from down there is a heavily sculptural gateway by Vignola (p. 46), with deep niches and thick rustication invading every element of the basement, and with muscly caryatids above them. That has been re-erected just around the corner. On the original site two pavilions still crown the hill (p. 47). They may well have been aviaries, buildings at the top dramatising the element of air. From them, staircases wrap around and down to the next level, where a huge, dripping, green, mossy beard of a fountain is sunk deep in a niche. From there you descend further ramps, moving inside the hill—from air to water to earth—to the dark cool of a cellar room. Below that, however, there is nothing now but the mess of excavation.

I have one last favourite in Rome itself. On the other side of the Palatine, overlooking the Circus Maximus, there is a wonderfully exuberant little house, a gimcrack fantasy built by some rococo eccentric in the early eighteenth century (p. 51). All he did was dress up his cottage with a loopy balustrade and windows which he must have modelled on his silver salvers.

The three oratories of
S. Barbara, S. Andrea
and St. Silvia in the grounds of S. Gregorio al Celio

44

an Giovanni Decollato. 1555

rosl.

Geranium

...der

palm

pear

Weedy Grass

1488. Institute for the official consolation of those condemn
1490 Innocent VIII approved institution   to death.
Church + oratory.
Cappella Maggione 1552 Altar pic Vasari

45

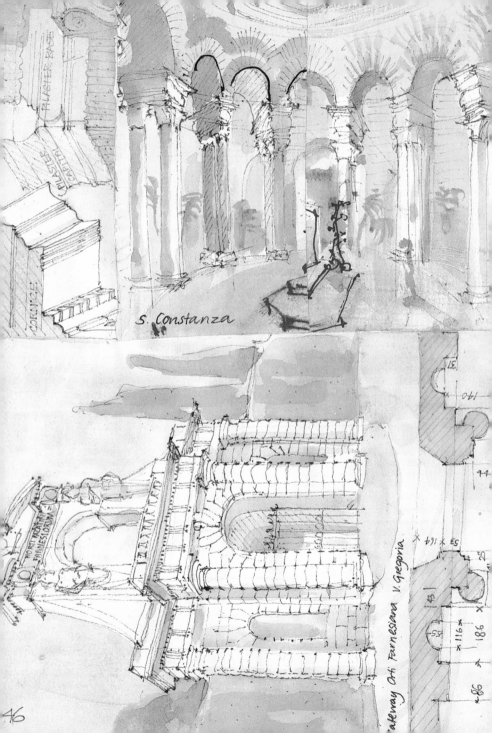

PILASTER BASE

PILASTER CAPITAL

CORNICE

PILASTER

S. Constanza

HORTI TRAIANI
PRAENESTORUM

allway off Farnesiana V. Gregoria.

31

140

44

25

53 × 164

43

116

186

58

86

46

Orti - Farnesiana plan + elevation

1:1 TOP BALLUSTRADE
ORTI FARNESIANA.

ORTI FARNESIANA
LOWER BALLUSTRADE

TEMPLE OF CL...

rusticated freeze.

Sermoneta

48

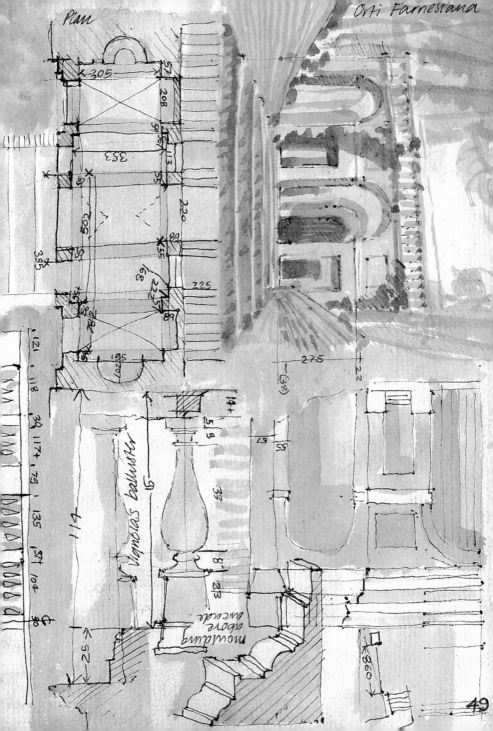

Plan

Orti Farnesiana

305
57
208
916
113
353
55
220
505
84
55
32
89
385
68
225
89
195

275
(38)
22

14+
5.9
9.1
6.7
55
33
Vignolas balustra
8
23

121
118
39
174
79
135
19
104
90
92

moulding above arcade

860

49

Ground

Grande...

...Galleria...

Piano Nobile.

Villa Doria Pamphili

Vedana

50

The Villa Madama (pp. 54–57) is halfway up the side of Monte Mario to the north of Rome. It is surrounded by woods and looks out over the countryside of the Tiber valley. When it was built in 1516, it was the first villa outside the walls of Rome, and this would all have then been virgin farmland. A Florentine cardinal, Giuliano de Medici, commissioned it from Raphael as a pleasure palace, a magnificent series of open courts and loggias intended for parties. It was open to the breezes from the east, which could blow through garden, court and loggia.

The great three-arch loggia, opening itself to the garden, was decorated by Raphael and his pupil Giulio Romano with delicate plaster reliefs, based on those they had seen in the ancient remains. The cool precision of the work and the painstaking attention to detail may well be something that appeals more to an architect than to a layman. But the rational organisation of interlocking spaces, axes and vistas can be appreciated by anyone. It is not difficult here to conjure up the ghosts of those warm renaissance evenings, the supper parties, the brilliant company.

But there is a tragic side to Villa Madama too. In 1527 Rome was sacked by the troops of the Emperor. Churches were looted, many were massacred and the Villa Madama was set on fire. From the Castel S. Angelo, where he had taken refuge, Giuliano de Medici, now Pope Clement VII, wept as he watched his villa burn. The High Renaissance was over, the years of optimism finished. The Villa, only half built when it was burnt, was never to be completed. The great nymphaeum and terraced garden which was intended to step up the slope of the hill behind was never made. Only one of the two wings in Raphael's plan, and only half of the great circular cortile which was to have been the open space between them, were ever built. It is there you now arrive, at the open arms of the curving façade, where the massive walls, in alternating tufa and Roman tile, with the column bases and capitals roughly boasted in travertine, have never been stuccoed.

Less than thirty years separate the building of the Villa Madama and the Villa Medici (pp. 58–59, 61), which is in a startling position

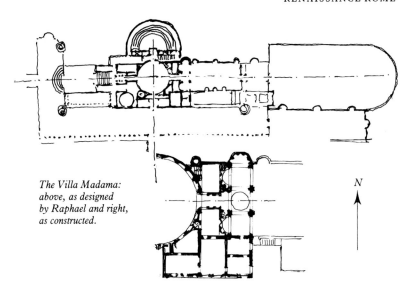

*The Villa Madama:
above, as designed
by Raphael and right,
as constructed.*

N

nearer the middle of Rome, with the whole city spread out at its feet. Its rear façade is the most charming, encrusted, like a fruit cake with almonds, in classical sculpture. The garden is thick with hidden places, gazebos and a conical mount among the sea of ilex and the strict lines of evergreen hedges. From the parapet there is an unforgettable view over Rome, a wide sweep hinged to the distant dome of St Peter's. Every spring the famous Medici Ball is held in this garden. All Rome is there in vastly elaborate fancy-dress; it's the great carnival day of the year. I went as a caryatid, with a pudding-bowl as a Doric capital precariously balanced on my head.

Rather enviably, the French Academy in Rome has been housed in the Villa Medici since the time of Napoleon. Lutyens's British School cannot compete on the same terms. But I had a consolation. The way into the middle of Rome from our School lies through the Borghese Gardens (p. 60). What originally was a series of baroque gardens was radically reshaped by a Scots painter, Jacob More, at the end of the eighteenth century in the English landscape style. Now it is dotted about with all sorts of neoclassical incidents.

Villa Madama.

54

Entrance Court.

cornice

A

cornice

simple architra

B

Architrave

B

D

E

Niche detail Orti Farnesina

C

C

D

Forte di Michaelangelo.
Bramante, Sangallo, Michaelang
1508 ———————⟶ 1535
Civitavecchia

Villa Madama

Villa Madama.

58

villa medici

59

In the Borghese Gardens.

leaves
sunlight.

Casino in the Bosco.
Villa Medici

S. Peters

Villa medici, Rome

61

Altarpiece Pienza Cathedral

Farmhouse at Cetinale, nr. Sienna.

62

From Lazio to the Po

ith the Scotts.

W HAT I like to remember more than anything else about the middle of Italy is how luxurious it can feel: staying in a villa with some friends, all of us painting and sketching, cypresses delineating every hill and with olive groves and little orange churches scattered below them. It was on a weekend like that I went to see the Villa Buonaccorsi (p. 66) and its glorious terraced gardens looking down over the Adriatic. It is in the Marche, where a beautiful sort of brick is the dominant material, and where fantastic church spires, obelisks and all sorts of quirky, mannerist details sprout up everywhere you look.

That is one side of it, but of course there are others. The kitchen of Fabrizio (p. 67), a friend of a friend, has all the unforced beauty of the peasant tradition. It is simple, not trying to be anything it isn't. The pots and pans hanging round the room, the fire, the kitchen stove, the logs stacked underneath, the bottle of Chianti hanging on one side, the beams, the terracotta tiles of the floor above—all the ingredients of coherence, integrity and charm are there, naturally achieving what self-conscious architects always strive to create.

On my journeys out of Rome I used to visit over and over again three renaissance gardens. There is no doubt in my mind that one, the Villa Lante (pp. 69, 71), is the most beautiful of the three. It was designed by Vignola in the 1560s and 1570s for a cardinal and I have often wondered what it is that makes it so perfect. It is certainly something to do with a sense of balance—between architecture and the living world, between stone and plants, between a respect for the natural and the amazing ingenuity with which water is made to run and tumble down the length of the garden, starting from the wild, oozy spring at the top and then falling through a series of fountains and water chains to the tight formality of the parterres at the bottom. The garden is somehow both cunning and restful, with wonderful ilex and plane trees roofing the terraces on which the water plays against the lichened stone. Even the fact that the villa is divided into two pavilions, the earlier of which, the Palazzina Gamberia, I drew, helps this air of coherence and rightness. Architecture does not dominate the garden; the garden is allowed to divide the architecture in two.

Villa Lante is Vignola's masterpiece. His pupil, Giacomo del Duca, worked on the slightly later garden at Caprarola (p. 73) only a few miles away. Up away from Vignola's palazzo there, beyond the chestnut wood which fringes the main garden, you can discover that most perfect of renaissance inventions, the *giardino segreto*. It is an island of order floating apart from the palazzo below, a satellite of solitude and perfection.

But there are strange and contradictory messages here too. The little *casino* at the top of the garden is a pure, even rather discreet building, with a straightforward Tuscan loggia. Here the President of Italy now comes to escape constitutional crises. But everything around it pulls in the other direction. Peacocks stalk and squawk past the architecture.

The walls of the deep corridor and staircases leading to the *casino* are encrusted with pumice and bearded with limestone. Giants too large for their beds are squashed up against a gigantic vase fountain, too large for its base. All around the *casino*, the herms, usually as straight as Grenadiers, turn to each other to chat and joke. It is all—and is surely meant to be—oddly unsettling. There is obviously wit here, as there is at Villa Lante, but no sense of ease. In both gardens the natural world has been picked up and played with, but the difference is this: at Lante the garden has extended the natural; at Caprarola it has gone against it.

No one knows who designed the garden at Bomarzo (p. 72), which is also not far away. It comes from the Gothic side of the renaissance imagination. If you are there alone at dusk on a winter's evening, it is a genuinely alarming place, with monsters and topsy-turvy houses rising out of the mist to greet you. Giant faces loom and leer out of the darkness. In a way, it bears the same relation to the Villa Lante as Michelangelo's *Last Judgement* does to the ceiling of the Sistine Chapel. Both the earlier works have a clarity and optimism and generosity about them, but Bomarzo, like the *Last Judgement*, is dark, chaotic and irrational. It is a place from which it is a relief to get away.

65

Chiostro · S. Nicola · Tolentino

Villa Buonaccorsi · m. Pescara.

66

Fabrizio's Tuscan Kitchen
S. Cesareo V. Porta S. Sebastiano

67

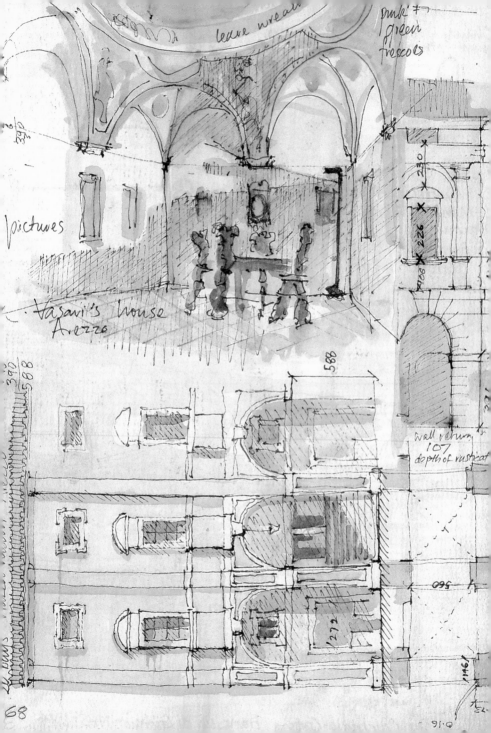

leave wreath

pink ?
green
frescoes

230

226

106

Pictures

Vasari's house
Arezzo

588

390
588

Wall return
107
depth of rusticat

588

095

272

68

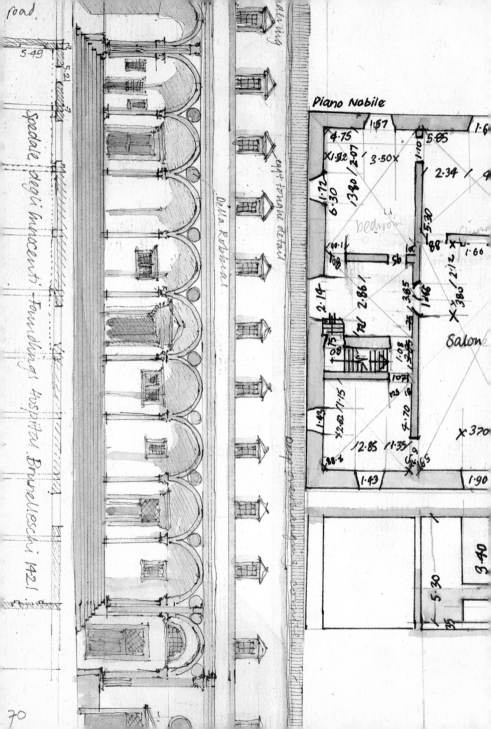

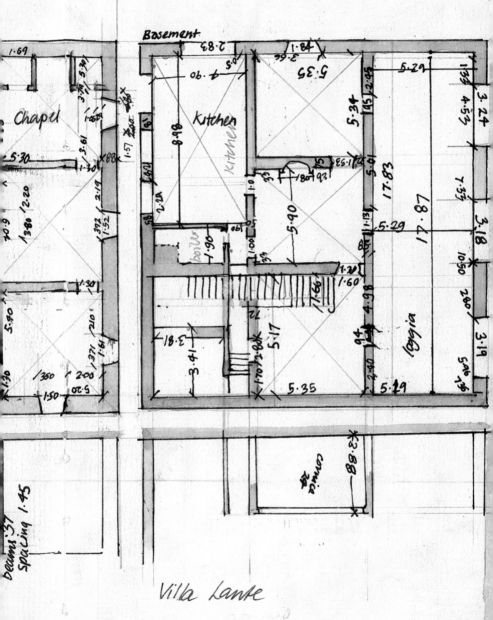

Basement

Chapel

Kitchen

loggia

Villa Lante

beams 37
spacing 1.45

71

Bomartzo

Caprarola

Casino in the giardino segreto - Villa Farnese
Caprarola.

ITALY has a genius for urban spaces. Whether it is the Piazza della Signoria in Florence (p. 76) or the space in front of the cathedral in Montepulciano (pp. 78–79), you always know that you have arrived. There is a natural rightness about Italian town planning which is quite absent from a country like England. Whenever an English town attempts something monumental in the centre it is usually a flop because the whole idea is rather foreign to the English. It may be partly to do with the weather—think how much these squares would lose if all the café tables and the restaurant awnings were tidied away. Even so, it must go deeper than that. It is something to do with towns mattering more to the Italians. In England the pattern has always been the grand country house with the little pied-à-terre in town. In Italy, it is exactly the opposite: the great urban palazzo and the small, if exquisite, villa in the country.

I sketched part of the Piazza Grande in Arezzo (p. 82) while a man regilded a picture-frame for me in a street just off to the side. It is one of the most extraordinary squares in Italy. Unnervingly, the whole square is on a steep slope, rather like Siena on a smaller scale, and you find yourself falling out of one corner. On every side, the square is full of the most contradictory buildings—medieval houses and a tower, the apse of a Romanesque church, the Palazzo Tribunale (with an early 18th-century façade), its eaves continuing uninterrupted over the half-medieval, half-renaissance Palazzo della Fraternità. Shoved into all of this, like a liner in a fishing harbour, is Vasari's huge Palazzo delle Logge, a classical arcade conceived on the grandest possible scale. Despite all these elements banging into each other head-on, the Piazza Grande (with its street-life of poodles, policemen and ladies covered in furs and too much scent) still works very well. It is one of the best examples I know of good architecture not submitting to its surroundings and still coming off.

Somewhere like Città della Pieve (p. 80) or Montepulciano works quite differently. In both these hill-towns, one made of brick, the other of a beautiful limestone, there is a sort of contained coherence. Everything hangs together. Of the two, Città della Pieve is the more homely, even naive, so that somehow, almost without thinking about it, it arrives at a playful, rococo prettiness. Everything is in brick—the castle and its machicolations, the palazzi and their rustications and above all the tall campanili, turned, shaped and chiselled like church candlesticks.

In Bologna (pp. 84–85), which tourists in Italy usually miss, there is a fascinating 16th-century redevelopment by Vignola. The point here is that, rather like Vasari in Arezzo, Vignola was regularising a rather higgledy-piggledy medieval side to the main piazza. His solution was very modern. He divided the block into two levels, the upper approached by a walkway above an arcade. This—four centuries early—was exactly what the modern movement would have come up with: a street in the air, away from the hubbub and mess, freeing up the space below.

Here in these pages too there is a sketch of the most astonishing room in Italy, Michelangelo's vestibule to the Biblioteca Lorenziana in Florence (p. 81). You saunter out of the cloister of S. Lorenzo, expecting nothing, wondering which way to go, and then suddenly fall over the doorstep into it. I've been there with a sensitive old soul who literally stood aghast at the threshold. Everything inside is back to front and upside down. Columns which should stand proud of the wall are sunk deep within it; pilasters taper towards the bottom and not the top; enormous volutes support nothing; large areas of wall remain completely blank. No one but Michelangelo could have created this. Walking into the room is like walking inside one of his own difficult, wrestling sculptures. Nothing is stable; everything conflicts with its neighbour. In the middle there is an amazing, cascading staircase which does not relate to the room around it in any way. It is as if it has been dropped into the space, where it has burst its skin and flooded outwards and downwards in wide undulations. There can be no other room in the world where the simple forms of architecture are so disturbing. Only the gloomy guardians, who hang around moping, cheerlessly telling you not to touch, can be indifferent.

illa acquired by Lorenzo's cousins 1477. Restored 1530
Garden laid out by Tripolo for Cosimo I, 1537.

lilac.   lilac.

Grotto

Bosco

Formal Parterre

orangery.

BOSCO

Villa Medici at Castello - Florenze

PIZZERIA

RISTORANT   CAVELL   FLORENZE

Piazza della

views archi-
       tecture

trompe l'oil
architrave

Vasari's House
Arezzo.

CONSORZIO FATA

a Florenze

77

Cathedral   Antonio Sangallo later Galli lea.

78

Piazza Grande · montepulciano
Palazzi by Antonio da Sangallo

Città della Pieve.

Bnzk.

80

Biblioteca medicea Laurenziana

Arezzo Tribunale Civile e Penale - Vasari's

The English College. 15 June 84
overlooking lake Albano

83

BOLOGNA

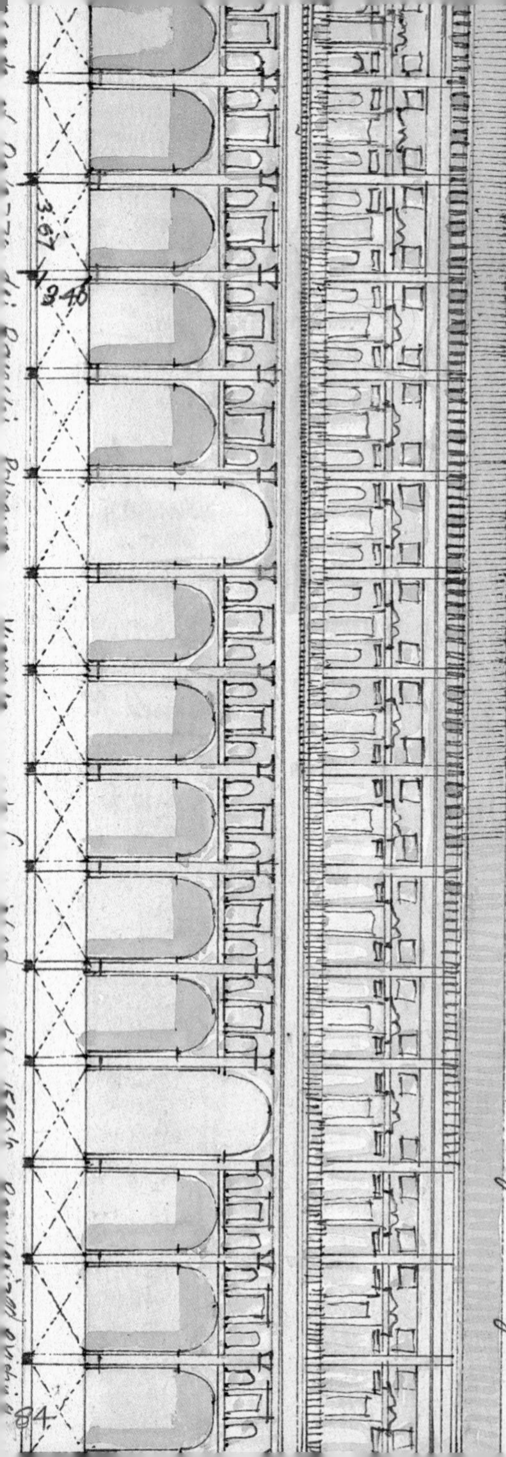
3.67
3.40

Facade of Palazzo dei Banchi, Bologna – Vignola

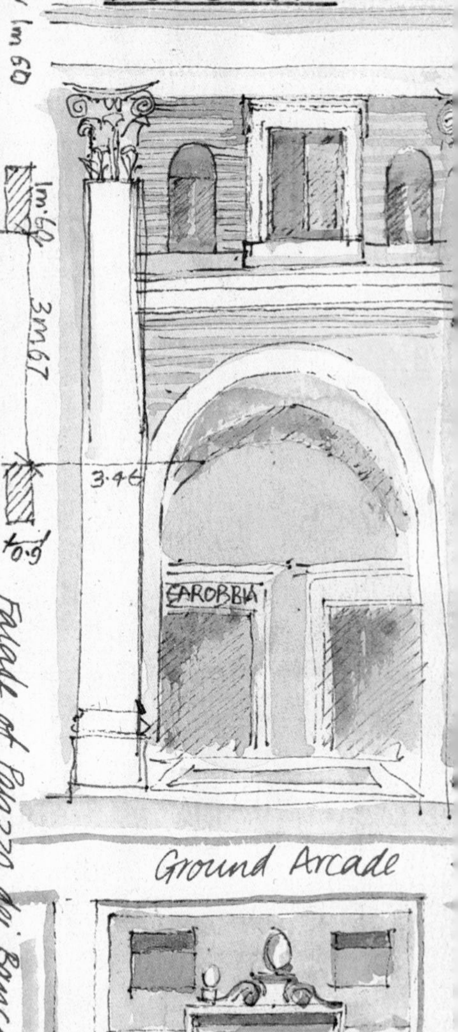
1m 60
1m·60
3m 67
3.46
0.9
CAROBBIA

Ground Arcade

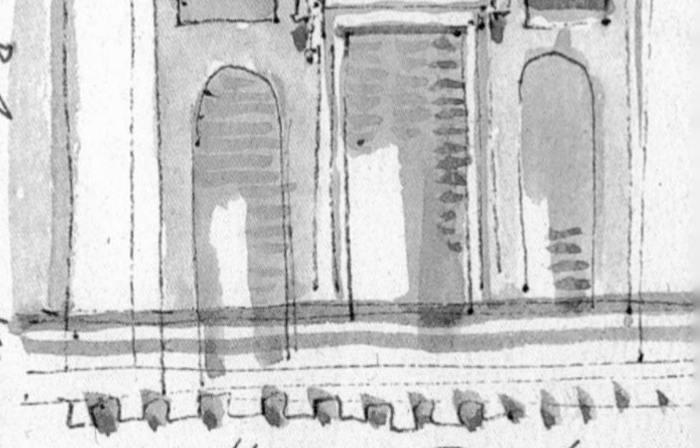

Upper Facade

gnolas Balldiuno S. Petronio

Arch recess 0.73 m

(0.9)

(1.8)

2.5   1.35   1   0.7

3.2

Palazzo Bocchi - Vignola
1545-55
Ground floor conforms to his design

Window Detail

Entablature of Door Porta
Palazzo Bocchi

capital   Architrave Frieze Cornice

minimum frieze width

85

ONE day I discovered a lovely church on the outskirts of Arezzo called S. Maria delle Grazie (p. 88). It is set apart in a grassy courtyard of its own and is surrounded by a tall and spacy loggia, designed by Bernadetto da Maiano in the 1480s, but very Brunelleschi in the way the entablature comes down as a sort of second capital above each column of the arcade. (It is rather like the Spedale degli Innocenti (p. 70) in Florence.) This and the wide Florentine eaves gives it an oddly and entrancingly oriental feel, almost like the Hall of Public Audience in the Red Fort at Delhi. A lot of it was redone by the Victorians but it is still beautiful—as clean and light and airy as a Fra Angelico.

That is the sort of architecture I like best—playful and inventive, but exact, careful. There is a fascinating contrast in Arezzo between this early arcade and a church by Vasari, the Badia delle SS. Flora e Lucilla (p. 89), in the middle of the town. It is much later, about 1565, and is far more precise in its use of classical vocabulary. Vasari

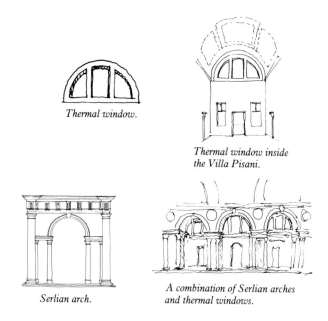

Thermal window.

Thermal window inside
the Villa Pisani.

Serlian arch.

A combination of Serlian arches
and thermal windows.

uses the triumphal arch motif, Serlian arches and thermal windows with a kind of academic formality that is in its way all too proper. Something has gone; it is a bit stodgy. And he has used two cross-axes in the plan so that you never know quite where you are.

Neither of those Arezzo churches can compare in the end with the flair of the great centralised churches just south of Arezzo at Todi and, above all, at Montepulciano. The church of San Biagio there (pp. 91–92), set out like a perfect model of itself on a grassy platform just below the town, is great architecture inside and out. The warmth of the honey-coloured stone, the one enormous centralised space of the church, exactly what Bramante and Michelangelo had in mind for St Peter's, the incredibly beautiful light inside—in all this the building is marvellously *consistent*. There is nothing about it of which you can say 'That lets it down.' Alberti defined beauty as 'a harmony of all the parts, fitted together with such proportion and connection, that nothing could be added, diminished or altered but for the worse.' San Biagio comes very close to that and almost more than anywhere else I know, you can really think here that, after the darkness of all those Italian Gothic churches, the European world is at last getting back to the light.

Santa Maria della Consolazione at Todi (pp. 92–93), which like San Biagio may well be derived from Bramante's scheme for St Peter's, belongs to the same family and is wonderful in its way, but is somehow a little lightweight, even spindly. What is so good about Montepulciano is the sheer mass of its bulk.

The way these churches are set away from their towns encourages one to look at them in this dramatic and total way, but of course most Italian churches are not like this. The experience of Italy itself is not like this. Most buildings, like the cathedral of Urbino (pp. 94–95), are pushed into their urban slots, surrounded by traffic, with bicycles leant up against them. The best way to see them—in fact the unavoidable and really enjoyable way of seeing them—is collapsed in a café opposite, exhausted by tourism, hardly registering superimposed temple fronts or the Palladian inheritance, and licking an ice cream.

ASA
IOSAPHAT
IORAM

S. Maria delle Grazie Arezzo
88 Bernadetto da majiano

145

Arezzo · Badia delle SS. Fiora e Lucilla

Serliana's + thermal windows   Trompe l'oit dome - Pozzo

sophisti-
cated

delicate

precision

Badia delle
S. Flora e
Lucilla
Reconstructe
1565 Vasar

Vasari 1565

Altar.

89

Prato.

S. Francesco Prato

Giuliano de
Sangallo · 1492

90

S. maria
delle
Carceri Prato.

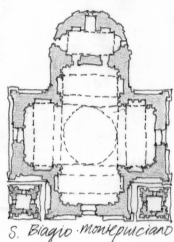

S. Biagio · Montepulciano

Il Tempio di San Biagio a Montepulciano.

Antonio da Sangallo begun 1518

91

montepulciano.

92

Todi

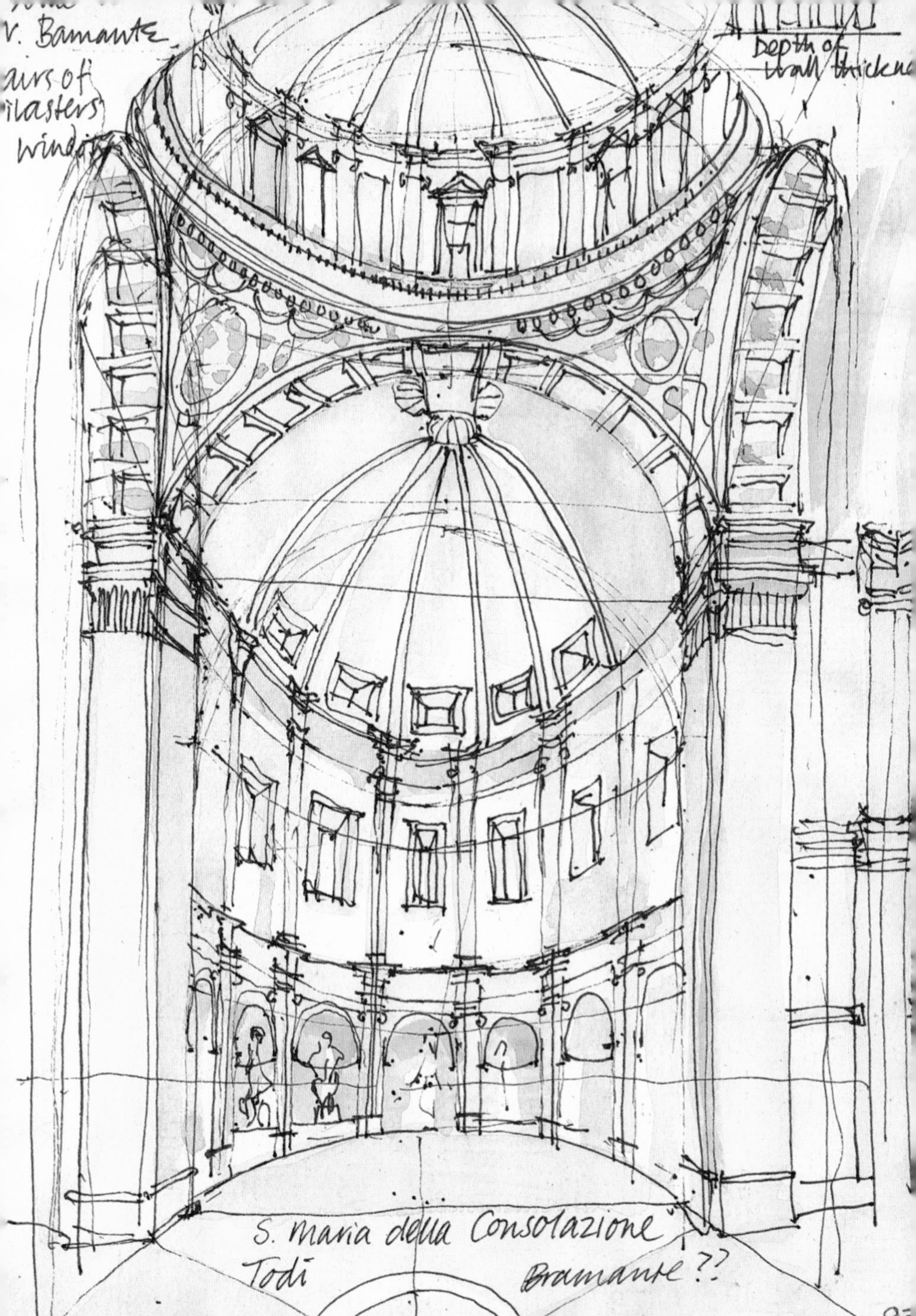

v. Bramante

airs of
ilasters
window

depth of
wall thickness

S. Maria della Consolazione
Todi   Bramante ??

93

Raphael's House
Urbino

Palazzo Ducale

94

Cathedral Urbino

The Veneto

villa Pisani - Bagnolo di honigo.

96

Palladio 1500-1580

Villa Barbaro-Maser

Villa Poiana - Poiana Maggiore

Plan
1570.

97

I spent a week or two in the Veneto playing the only game that the English have played there since the seventeenth century—Hunt the Villa. It is daunting to begin with—so many villas scattered so obscurely across such a wide slice of Italy—but then that is the fun of it—chasing the next villa before the sun goes down, arriving after dusk, finding the gates locked and the ever-present Dobermanns snarling behind them, turning away disappointed, being called back by the housekeeper, the Marchesa is away, and then, in a perfect recreation of the eighteenth century, the private tour around the house, the tall geometry of the rooms, with the assortment of modern conveniences tucked in discreetly (in this loggia the Queen Mother had lunch only last summer, here the Germans destroyed the frescoes in the final days of the war) and then the tip, the goodbye and the drive to pasta in the restaurant next to the Basilica in Vicenza.

What you soon realise is that Palladio in Italy is not at all like Palladio in England or America. Somehow when his architecture is transported abroad it becomes effete and too classy. Here in the mist-ridden, agricultural Veneto he is much more obviously part of the place, at heart an indigenous architect. Here as you breeze past farm after farm you suddenly realise that every barn looks Palladian. In all this, in the balance of windows, in the confident arrangement of architectural masses, you can see some of the sources of the Palladian style. In this way Palladio is a local architect. His villas could never have been built by a Roman.

If you go to Lonedo, on the first foothills of the Alps north of Vicenza, you will find there two Palladian houses, the Villa Godi (p. 100) and the Villa Piovene (p. 100), within a couple of hundred yards of each other, bridging the whole Palladian era. Godi was the first villa Palladio worked on in the late 1530s, Piovene the last in the 1570s. The extraordinary thing is that Villa Godi is by far the more radical of the two. It is modern and abstract like early Le Corbusier. He has cast the architectural orders aside and devoted himself to space, pattern-making, and the break-up of window and wall. In classical terms this is an astonishingly exciting facade; seen in the

The Villa Godi.

vernacular tradition of the Veneto, it is simply a very clear example of what was being done anyway.

The Villa Piovene, just up the hill, was probably commissioned by a rival family to those living in the Villa Godi. A second-rate motive produced a rather second-rate building. It is so uninventive that many people think it cannot have been designed by Palladio himself but by his follower Scamozzi. But Villa Piovene is interesting because it shows how a house designed by formula will never really work. Put up a rectangular box, add a couple of wings with colonnades, slap on a temple front, with stairs up to it, and there you have it—the Palladian Villa. It does not work like that. Villa Piovene is leaden, which houses by Palladio himself never are. This is the other side to Palladio: he is constantly inventive, almost never repeating a solution to a problem, endlessly shuffling the elements to hand to produce new patterns, new ways of flattering his patrons at relatively little expense, new ways of producing that cool, harmonious balance in a building which we all, intuitively, recognise to be right.

Villa Godi 1537-42 Lonedo.
Battista del Moro

1516
49
Godi
23
56

Degg + tongue

Villa Piovene . Lonedo

100

Villa Comero - Piombino Dese.

Villa Emo
Fanzolo

Villa Emo.

Villa Foscari - Malcontenta

101

Cushion 7.

Leopoldine Esterhazy
1810 Terracota.

Villa Saraceno · Fi

Sunday morn · Café Soraru
The Basilica · Vicenza.

102

Amore e Psiche
1787

anova Museum.
r. Bassano.

Andromeda
1818/19

li Aquqliaro

Villa Badoer - Fratta Polesine

103

THE Palladian villas, or most of them, were farms. At some, like Villa Barbaro at Maser (p. 96), this is rather difficult to believe. It is one of the most sophisticated houses on earth, decorated by Veronese with wonderful frescoes of the rural landscape seen through the frame of painted arches and balustrades. One has to accept on trust that cows walked about in the arcaded wings to each side. But many of the other villas are still obviously agricultural. At Villa Emo (p. 101), only a few miles from Maser, the usual steps up to the main portico have been replaced by a ramp, which is said to be much easier for horses to climb.

There is one villa in particular which brings this home. Villa Saraceno (pp. 102–3) is at Finale, a few miles south of Vicenza. It is now little more than a farmyard. The house with its plain, rather clumpy three-arched loggia is deserted, with steaming piles of golden muck in the arcaded *barchessa* to one side. The garden is a ploughed field. It's a wonderfully melancholy place! But then you notice one thing which makes it different from any other semi-ruined Italian farm: all over the ploughed field are the footprints of loyal Palladio fans—out to get a good look at the rear facade (rather a confused mess like many of the villas), back again and over the crumbling wall, in through a broken window and then across the dust and rubbish inside the deserted house right up to the attic on the top floor. The attic is lit, according to Vitruvian principles, by the large grilled windows intended to provide plenty of ventilation on this granary floor to stop the weevil getting into the wheat. Here it is in all its simplicity: the Palladian villa as the farmer's house—well made, without too much detailed stonework (which would have cost too much), at home in its landscape, with a settled and horizontal air, the architecture of stability and acceptance. No wonder it appealed to the English!

You can take this too far. Palladio cannot really be called the farmer's architect. He works on rather more levels than that. He can appeal to the academic just as much as to the amateur. Like Mozart, his architecture can seem deceptively easy, his cool, suave certainty in some ways rather obvious. It does not really matter whether you are aware or not of his strict proportional system or the tight interlocking of its elements. Either consciously or intuitively you get the same message from the best of his villas—clarity, intelligence, no anxiety, nothing shifty, the civilised thing at ease with itself.

It is true that many of his buildings don't quite fit with this idea. There is the extraordinary Villa Serego at Santa Sofia di Pedemonte (p. 108) with its rusticated columns like stacks of tyres or the legs of a Michelin Man—an 'unpalladian building' but undoubtedly by Palladio. Even the most famous and influential of all, the Villa Rotonda (p. 106) outside Vicenza, is rather more theatrical than settled, with its show-off porticos on all four sides, one of them, rather absurdly, facing a sheer drop. But if I had to name a single villa which does embody Palladianism for me, I would choose the Villa Poiana (pp. 97, 107) at Poiana Maggiore a few miles south of Vicenza. Only the central block was built (in the 1550s), but it has a boldness and rigour which takes it out of its time. He uses a motif invented by Bramante in his Nymphaeum at Genazzano (pp. 34–35)—the Serlian arch and above it five round holes punched into the stone. But here the idea is reduced to its absolute geometric minimum, excluding all fuss or elaboration. Palladio distils architecture, cools it down, even boils it down, to its essential bones. The effect is not brutalist—there is delicacy in it—but it *is* almost unapproachably pure.

Thinking about my year in Italy, I find the Renaissance forking in front of me. From Bramante, who represents to me some sort of unity and perfection—I am thinking of the Tempietto—two routes diverge. One, through Michelangelo, Giulio Romano and the Mannerists moves on to the baroque and the rococo, an architecture of complication and movement. The other goes in the opposite direction, stabilising, simplifying, purifying, flowers in Palladio and then northern Palladianism, to peak again in neoclassicism and eventually the modern movement. These are the two poles of architecture. I am not sure which to prefer. Perhaps there is no need to choose.

Gk tetrastyle hall

Villa Pisani - Montagnana. 1542

La Rotonda 66-67

'06

Villa Pojana, Pojana Maggiore 1548

Teatro Olimpico. Vicenza.

107

Villa Trissono.

Palazzo Valmarana 65

108 Villa Serego, S. Sofia di Pedemonte.

S. Bernadino Verona, San Michele.

Palazzo Barbaran de' Porto 69?
Vicenza.

Palazzo Thiene

Palozzo
Thiene
Vicenza

City walls Verona San Michele.
Porta Paleo 1548?

Capitals - Villa Serego

109

Villa Pisani Bagnolo. Vicenza 41-44.   Vn PIS

sima recta
cassetto
corona
marmo
pietra
ferchiarone

IL Redentore

110.

The main hall.

Sitting room

3a

7
15

Redentore from garden

S. Giorgio · Entrance

Refectory S. Giorgio

111

Index

Page numbers in **bold** refer to illustrations